Stem

PRINCETON SERIES OF CONTEMPORARY POETS

Rowan Ricardo Phillips, *series editor*

For other titles in the Princeton Series of Contemporary Poets, see the end of this volume.

STELLA WONG

Stem

POEMS

PRINCETON UNIVERSITY PRESS
Princeton & Oxford

Published by Princeton University Press
41 William Street, Princeton, New Jersey 08540
99 Banbury Road, Oxford OX2 6JX

press.princeton.edu

All Rights Reserved

Library of Congress Cataloging-in-Publication Data

Names: Wong, Stella, author.
Title: Stem: poems / Stella Wong.
Description: Princeton: Princeton University Press, 2024. | Series: Princeton series of contemporary poets
Identifiers: LCCN 2024012587 (print) | LCCN 2024012588 (ebook) | ISBN 9780691264042 (paperback) | ISBN 9780691264035 (hardback) | ISBN 9780691264059 (e-book)
Subjects: LCGFT: Poetry.
Classification: LCC PS3623.O59837 S74 2024 (print) | LCC PS3623.O59837 (ebook) | DDC 811/.6—dc23/eng/20240325
LC record available at https://lccn.loc.gov/2024012587
LC ebook record available at https://lccn.loc.gov/2024012588

British Library Cataloging-in-Publication Data is available

Editorial: Anne Savarese and James Collier
Production Editorial: Theresa Liu
Text and Cover Design: Pamela L. Schnitter
Production: Lauren Reese
Publicity: Jodi Price and Carmen Jimenez
Copyeditor: Jodi Beder

Jacket illustration by Ilya Milstein

This book has been composed in Garamond Premier Pro

10 9 8 7 6 5 4 3 2 1

FOR MY MOTHER AND MY GRANDMOTHER

CONTENTS

Stem

Dramatic Monologue as Beatriz Ferreyra

This is some decomposed music. This
is some double. O great

and terrible pressing! Submerged
in the memoriam swamps

I want to catch your thin neck full
bodied breath in the blue

funeral vase, your death
masked. This is like that

satanist music where they
play it backwards. So I've heard.

On a List of Games That Buddha Would Not Play, Number 1 [He Abstains from Robbery]

Once I watched a screen-ready trilogy
of deer graze my front yard

in Iowa, only by the blobbed bulbs
of their eyes in the dark.

In the dark, our eyes have the rods to see
only in black and white.

A triad: a father, son, and some
downed spirit. Forgiven in trespass.

I need to stress
the pacifist element here.

I did not see the deer frozen
in the middle of the road

nor strike one with my car
because I am not a white poet

writing about the same deer
for two centuries.

Even if I had struck, my car is not
a Volvo, evolved to survive

striking a full-grown moose,
ramming its legs full-speed

and getting crushed by its body, for
Swedish and Canadian drivers

only. For even if I had killed it,
my non-existent gun is not

a Glock, intelligently designed to fire even
if the muzzle

is stuffed with sand. That's only "merciful
bullet" in McGuffin.

You share your hazing rituals
about panicking and grabbing

a picnicking doe, set
in concrete. A kettlebell of a deer,

when the ask was to bring back gnomes.
True story, staggering

as Sisyphus under his boulder of faith
in privilege. The most stressed

test: where to leave the carcass
in the dark frat-house basement. How to care for

the metallic scratches it left on your brother's car.
Which mechanisms are built to survive.

Here we go, you'll say, the race card
I've never played. Here's to the poem of gray areas

I've never written. Here
we've bitten the bullet.

Need

Your right knee is a haunted staircase.
Your left is a spring-breaking

island. Your knee is a moving
snowplow. Your kneecap is a Mona Lisa

fridge magnet. Your knee linkage
unlike a shrimp tail.

Your leg skin is an ice-ray
Chinese lattice design. Recursive shape

grammar. Your left
kneecap is the black leather Star

Wars helmeted special edition
Mr. Potato Head. The antihero. The reflex.

Hammer it and the knee's ear falls off
to no response. There, there—

The State That Replaces Religion Doesn't Want to Adopt a Dog with Me

As I grow older I like looking at chaos
like the Westminster shows. You fight me
with your omniscience—dogs who look like dogs
are bred that way. Like I'm supposed to love

a rescue who looks like a wormhole
opened up in the evolutionary tree. Don't call me
Noah, or some kind of dog park pervert.
I use videos of glossy-haired weiners

eating raw meat as ASMR
to fall asleep. Duck hearts and chicken necks are all part
of the deal. You love all ten hours
of video showing a mangy biter,

a clotheshorse chained to a fence since God
knows when. Bloodhounds have their ears
to make a cone for their noses so they scent
by following the ground

instead of smelling out. Just for the threat of it,
we're who the other wants
as a pet. So it's true you've saved me. But don't
forget, this mouth could swallow you whole.

Dramatic Monologue as Laurie Spiegel

Sure it sounds like a dog in a prairie,
not the prairie dogs that say Steve

but little prairie synths. They're
synthing through the tall synth grass,

the color you see when you press on
your closed eyelids. It's the sound of sewing together

synth rags into a quilted synth
and shaping whatever speaker you want. Pretty

much the sound of cold synth boiled
over a synth bonfire. Powerlessness doesn't sound

like this. Now, who's interposing is this country
being born, and if

synth versus analog tug-
of-war will win.

Modular systems are just
like log cabins. Random

access is taking the first bite
off a dish in the kitchen and getting away

or even better, cooking up your own
technician. Eating the synth scraps,

what they call a chef's treat. When
you don't have a nested hierarchy,

truly synthetic, then the synth is person-personal,
the synth is built. The self wanders in and out.

American Horror Story

Let me tell you how I make myself
appear / more likeable, less likely

to eat your pet. Your neighbors
would rather choke / their puppies out

by the collar / like a fellow white
belt / on the jiujitsu mat / digging

knee bone and boner. / They know
what it means / to mount a little

too long. There are other children before me
driven here / for the festival

of music and wine. / The family eats up
the little homeless girl / who sleeps under her

grand piano. My grand dame of a teacher
played for the Kennedy administration

back when the story was Camelot / and now the story is
well hold on a minute.

Someone plays I'm in heaven
and it's heaven / for whoever pays.

I'm in Aspen / named after the silver dollars
the leaves resemble. Money / does grow

on trees for a rich person, / a little artificial
waterfall outside / one living

room window, different trees in each picture /
gingerbread pane. Two dead /

ringers for Ming dynasty foo dogs.
The hostess frames her life

story, gripping / my little finger
with her non-baccarat hand.

Every grapple / is over / submission
in this world / outside control

of the opponent's collar, sleeves, and belt
are all fair / play. I am caged

by her button eyes. I am baby / fat
enough to call my mom, mommy. As a child /

therapist, the hostess saw a boy my age / with a stray
he fed, snored with, and loved.

One day it was gone, full stop /
and her sentences stop. She looks down on me

asking if I know why / the family had enough
food to eat the next day.

One little bone. Two real foo.
A wood-burning oven. Who orders whom.

In jiujitsu, the body is a table / a torso
and posts. Riddle me this.

Gamely I ask what's next, / and in that
order / I learn / in the eyes of witches

some children are crumbs / to brush off.
You bet she doesn't serve

carbs as hors d'oeuvres / and
what kind of child relishes mini pickles

and other small-hearted sour foods?
This is why / Gretel starves

rather than contort / in a box.
Poor girl. Poor boy.

The witch lives / happily.
You ask if this is a real story. All of them

are true / crime shows,
even if I tell them like a bitch.

Dramatic Monologue as
Johanna Magdalena Beyer

This is some hard music
to listen to. My Dutch clogged
name. What you've heard about me is

whom I've predated. Some of it hostile
and probably not well-informed. Some of it
mediated. As a port's port,

I have my baby like a mushroom,
pinning away for
my own logged arrhythmic growth.

My developing chestnut nubs.
My coup d'épée as king
oyster. The spongy spores are all ready

there. I am an ever-changing
something. A sprouted hair.

Dramatic Monologue as Wendy Carlos

I do prefer cyberpunk
mermaids because they're realistic

in terms of rust and advancement.
Not impossible to attain. Yes, it is

the tech of the future but the windows are grimy,
the hyperspeed button falls off,

and the shipwreck's hinges squeak. I
have a beautiful self-image

as the girl from the ring, with my hair chandelier
pretty as a batik, forbidding

designs of humans and animals.
So, the tuba footfalls of a giant. The

melting Gothic castle. The party is
over when the dirge dregs. The best

things to score are
like us, unnumbered.

Briny

You are the sea
creature. If you feel sad,

I can eat you. Wisdom is all men
fighting algae. The gears

are bleak-roasted, and helpless.
I think black water chestnuts

are best sounding.
Your feet are the corallines

of New York Harbor,
nannofossils and current

unattached specimens.

Hyperpersonal Dramatic
Monologue as Holly Herndon

I am the only hope in any other / guilt
banners asking for your / maximal maximal /
church offering. To pay the surround / in eight choirs. Please, think
    of the self

surveillance my partner required. I recorded the pet ouroboros /
ate / bookended / Möbius stripped / just had an all-around
naked voiced weekend. Monsterly kitsch / is full of what

my medusa—with renaissance / hair rumbles. I have
a funnel of conditioner to waist /
and a pallet glamour / and something to locket / with

—draws as blue foliage. / Meaning, eyelashes of the foregrounded /
azure leaves. The polyphylla is striped like a renaissance
slash / sleeve. At the very least, it sounds like / I am a scarab.

No scabs against the strike. Here / lie /
parameters, squeezed between
the red queen / and the hoopla / of church. There's no boundary

but boundary. How are things? The usual, snakily /
into the extramusical / lying outside the province / of music. Ad
banners for attack / and decay / triggers / to Velcro again.

Dissection

JA teaches me (it's my choice) to cut
out the heart / of the emo tomato.
(With consent.) / My high school chemistry /

professor was kicked off / every jury
she tried to duty on / because she had no
fingerprints / from burning them off /

on Bunsen burner hot plate testing.
She's excited one / of the cats we had /
delivered in formaldehyde was pregnant.

Triplets. On the subway / PSA, three faces say stop
the spread, wear a mask. One says not quite /
with the nose out. Someone has slapped

their sticker / life begins
at conception and in small font /
and ends with planned parenthood. / When I was little

and things were unplanned, a stranger hosted me and made me /
lasagna because all children, even foreign bodies,
love lasagna. I hated tomatoes back /

then. The pool / swimming across the street / like a blue gem, a
    round cap
of a formaldehyde / jerry can. Things were different then.
She was a silk painter / and worked for planned parenthood, which
    helps

families plan when they want children . Years later
my bioethics professor / find him on tv /
pops out like a pregnant belly's button. / He's the mean principal

on the Simpsons. / Does a double take
spotting / me sleeping in the front row like a good
girl he shows / a tomato seed swimming

in tomato jelly / and calls it
anti / life and I will always throw up in
my mouth / at the sight of human

blood. (Any blood.) / Anyway
the sticker next to it is a super hot Satan
so sign me up! Evangelicals / doing their work huh.

He really didn't hold office / hours of nothing for us.

Response to a Tracklist from God Quarantining with His Ex

To get around
human resources and chivalry, God,
I ask you to the track every fortnight, and without fail

you fail to respond. Our first and last run
the park sends down biblical rain. Then there
is a hole in your slowly flooding sneaker's toe. Thanksgiving

in a pandemic lockdown, you say you'll fly
into a wildly racist state
or a wildly racist and bath-salt-snorting puppy-eating crocodile state.

It's a full-time Job when I'm not upright, bearing
your tracklists of rock and rollers and other high
priests who destroyed followers in the name of love.

You love your dog so much you're two bus stops away
from your ex's house to be nearby when
the apocalypse and the takeout get here

which really shows me my place.
I'm accusing you like Satan.
When Christmas rolls around you'll see

if you have dog-sitting duties. Now she vacations in a global
    quarantine.
The shots you've fired off from her empty place—the unfamiliar
    floors
are powerfully white, I simply cannot explain it.

Like Florida, I'm an unfamiliar battleground
and on mimosa Sundays, your old pet isn't even cute, though
animals domesticated early as wolves look defenseless

to survive. They always look back,
then forward, then back up at their humans. Needy,
but I feel that. Yours freezes and points at rabid squirrels—it tracks

so hunters could tell where pheasants fell from the sky. The climate-
    change denier tells
me couples adopt dogs to prepare for their future
children. Another kind

of plague. You ask why you weren't invited to my birthday
and God, I'm just so tired, especially in your adverse
conditions, of running after you.

Ars Poetica

Your six pack like a Wonder
Bread peanut butter jelly.
Your nose like a saltine cracker,

son of hardtack. Your dad's
heart attack at your age now.
Your hair like a teddy bear

from the fancy toy store
with nutcrackers at the door.
Your skull like the genre

that is Toto from Dorothy's basket,
but in fact not Toto. Like the Scottish
terrier. Your face like an oblong fact,

a rectangle. Like a secret service
agent but regular,
a beauty when you wait for me

like a lamppost, solo and grim. Your chin
you'll never shave again,
not after the Bermuda cruise ship.

How you clean up
the crossword in 1980s haberdasher
terms. You're always scared

everyone's looking at you
but can I just say,
I always am. Isn't that worse.

Dramatic Monologue as Mira Calix

You know when you're one of the ones they used
to work the pilot light or the sax at the blade

runner clubs when you glitch in neoprene
and reject the capitol, capitalism

and neon tube all caps. Really. What's in a right
click? Glowing ball-joints or peeping

potato eyes. The stubby sacks don't know what externality's going
to come up. Are notoriously bad at concertina

and guessing. Don't remember the contrapposto,
the negative space. The dappled beats.

On a List of Games That Buddha Would Not Play, Number 18

Manesika   guess these thoughts
no one else calls me   habibti
I could never   hold a fan   like you
        of an electric blue   something
something   with plumes   with a
folded paper plate   scallop shaped
and what a Venusian one too
or I'm mis-recalling   can't hold a
candle to   the real thing   it was
in all a very hot day, sweating
beers with very hot   people, one
non-binary   with fishnets,
shitkickers and a twiddly

mermaid do   in a dorm   room at a
school   named university of
spoiled children   we were not
aware of the fact   we would not
have them   yet, waving to   and fro
for some top   100s song   90s
song   maybe 80s song   I wouldn't
        know I was never   popular by
that same definition   things you are
        at a barbecue   in the desert
uncle   the son   of a
mother who is   safe and healthy
that's the best
smoker I know   always off to see a
wizard   always on   the green brick
        road to quitting   any way I have
wandered enough

                    The docks
are gone now   the boards un-
planked   but the pylons are still
planted   little choirs   in
wooded testament   rooted so deep
    that removal would rake mud
and pollute the stream   you must
recall   we got nothing   but the
director's head   we got him banned
from campus   from stepping foot
here

    I'm sorry   to hear   those boys
called you a slut   that is   a typo
they called you   a slur
I only wish   it had   been
about the cigs   or said flags
you and I both   don't swear
that way   hold me back   don't
let me fight   without you   can
your allegiance   for the new
year be to never   quit

                    I fired you and
everyone else up   I fired me too
from the board   look over the
footless mermaids   ambitious
driven pylons   how prescient—
dashing   as they are   wrecking
ships   taking names   calling out
the man at the helm   and didn't
Odysseus avoid his fate?   But isn't
that old hat   fishing

              isn't the villain still
out there?   Returned the following
      time re-formed, unreformed
when he tongue-lashed you   for
smiling   him to his doom?
The sirens were half   bird half body
      interpretations of womanhood
really, don't!   have two feet to
stand on   we're clawed   winged
scaling   the power structure   can't
we mudrake   like this too?

This   is my promise   I'll hold
the line like your baby   nephew Sanad
reeling in   a fishing rod   of your
dreadlock   and maybe most   likely
lovingly biting down.   Where else
but down   in our rawest forms
are we most dreaded?   What else
could I want   but to open fire?

Batshit

I want to say something
about horses but my family is watching

a horror show of screaming violins,
ghoulish trumpets, and a drumbeat for

a heart. It's come
to the day we knew would come, and maybe it's the end

of the engagement or the storied
chivalry I'd built

up in my head. And I'm turning back
to celibacy, to climbing the cloisters

alone and thinking about monkhood
among the poison plants, the first sign

in Eden, to drawing the worst possible
bats, in nubby lead pencil, with human faces, the kind

of smile that only
babies can smile. There will be a lot more now. Not ours.

Bottom

As a barred hamlet would,
or a greater soapfish,

the steely-eyed elevator door cries
and the steel-nerved radiator leaks radiator

fluid. And sometimes piss.
A solitary hunter

in limited territory,
feeder, masked, butter, black.

Scorpion W2

You want to join the army
but you've aged out

and I think that's pretty reasonable
given what I know of war

from the things they carried / everyone
in that world is barely legal

from black-and-white movies
and stories / from the bow-tie professor

how his town's post office man stares
down his birthday boy pal until he signs

up for the draft. I imagine this too
takes place / in black and white.

You're too pretty
to war with, but that's what we play at

week after week. Friendly fire
like you should always watch your back

around girls who look / barely legal.
After college, your prized possession

should be owning / your own
washing machine /

or a good pickup truck
with the back that comes down

or if you live / in the country
and want to make / lady friends, the professor says

a ladder's the best pickup line. Also that
winter shadows are blue, if you look / accurately.

I just want to wake up with you, and up /
for anything, is how you sell your profile

until it gets delisted from inaction.
You are down

for the count / after garlic toast, warmed
corn tortillas, complex

carbohydrates or other issues
taking on / some color.

The times I grill
you. The things you carry / on

the subway include a survival pack,
first-aid kit, bulletproof board, knives,

a pen (weaponized) and two
flashlights (weaponized). One

of my grandfathers fought
in the Second World War. Which theatre? I don't know

how combatants recognize each other
out of uniform. I'd like to think

the reason you don't come back is your belief
the duty

of any captured soldier is to try
to escape.

False Pink Reds Translate No Good Wins

How to stay happy / how to stay
silent / how to
stay alive / how to stop

thoughts / Cavendish is the new
monoculture / the new pink banana /
the new red banana / banana hearts
are made / of twenty hands / deal

this deck / how to play / well / what do you want
to play / in a pandemic, no snow days /
play unwell / how to find snow

banana / how to find false banana /
how to find radioactive banana / how to be

less / autistic / how to translate
English to Chinese / how to translate
obsessive / the poem is getting away
with something / who are the bad

odds you and I share / a birthday /
how to get away / with Latin
the dead language / the dead speakers.

On a List of Games That
Buddha Would Not Play

Akkharika / guess / at the words
written on the back / the image /

I took of you / when I needed a win /
for an assignment / is seedy, grainy

and lavender. Some kind of blue
valentine. Your spinal cord is

the pomological / high
society fruit. The poet whose poems /

are shredded / not one /
collection left,

tattooed on your left shoulder
blade. The future is funny /

in ancient Greek,
which Greeks can't read. Insert

a line here about the distance /
between the word and the idea of it.

In the gray marble / bathroom, I want you to look / back
and we really did / these

things in our youth.
You grow more beautiful

things and words for things. Crowning
the big spindled sun

-flower. The laureled
green-white strawberry /

under wraps / under humicubation /
like a rumor. Over-seeded just so /

like an ovary / should have / been.
Hades' hell fruit. The British version /

is sometimes monstrous / from what I
look up. The shower myths make the form /

and background / cold and beautiful. /
Before we are in stem

we steam / your roots
and red layers.

In circulation / most plants
are not true / to name.

My male friend's dad says sow wild oats / and true
to form / I don't remember why / we did

these things / but I was glad
to be there with you /

in witness / in the grainy time.

Manifold

I like your body / which you don't find
hot / and I like that about you.

Me, a weepy lettuce / purply, nutrient deficient
scrunchy / hyperbolic plane

which you say maxes out surface
area / superficial / same in Latin.

An alumna suggests findom / though it sounds
like call girl / with bank receipts.

The hyperbole form is desperate
to escape / from me. Where

else / can you find my body / type
in cacti / coral / kelp

sponge / maybe pouty calla lilies
would help / meaning vaginas / hail

the giant / one in times square / literal
center of the universe / super face

made out of magenta / acrylic
nails / gemstones and you can't find it

online. On your shoulder, I make brassy
trombone raspberries / we like to watch / men fold

men are lost / inside, called it
a carapace / and a hot pink

metallic fountain. On top / it's fluted. No
really, the universe is a hyperboloid.

Of all the multidimensional / spaces,

bloopers, crying / through
this orchestra is hijinks enough.

Dramatic Monologue as Pauline Oliveros

What are you picking up? A lot of pink
noise and feedback. Even the punishment

is a square. The good doctor is trying to help
but you were born on a Wednesday.

The blue opera alien is singing
rubber again. Under the dictator's hip of trazodone,

the dreams got worse. The ashen Cinderella
dresses in the mood you're getting.

More waking, more lizard drips.
The wolves are unsettled by the consistency

of your screaming. They can only be indicative
of deep rooted trauma. Deep as potato tubers.

Just as hairy. We're all forked
as storage organs. Time to get us in the ground.

Colony

The algae is growing like Gatorade
stains. It's lucky to write bad

poems. Like driving a short tractor
into a utility pole / in Mongolia. What

are the odds we're both unwanted
mistakes? The algae is growing like a

bad poem. The maximal utility function leaves
no one / full. Mongolia stays unwanted

after its short, odd escapades. Over
the elegiac green pee stain

we go. This poem is full / of mistakes. It
must be / the luckiest to survive.

Dramatic Avowals as Sophie

Singing Vietnamese karaoke before the jury
lets teal-haired Orpheus bring back her wife.

She sends a video from the salon.
My crossword answers

are sheik, cloud and party.
All the big fun letters, Cyber Monday

getting medieval. At my age,
she had a vasectomy so it's okay

today's answer, undue, is not a word.

Keeper

Purple-haired Orpheus is kind
of a lapsed Catholic. After Argentina's two goals,

she invites me to Christmas carols at St. Paul's Church.
The goofy one, she says, who didn't even know

Jesus. She knows the names of the others,
thanking her cats and siblings on the same line, like Good Will

Hunting and his twelve big brothers.
All those almost-vowels. So many endings with y.

Farewell My Cucumber

—after Cybele by Mihail Chemiakin

My cucumber has many breasts
to speak of and speak through.

Some are knowledge fountains,
which are just upside-down faucets.

Some nipples spark with conflict
luckily unlike corporate wars

but more like my cucumber's self.
A creepy vine. Some are fonts

of milk, sans serifed or cursive.
Mostly water, when spiraling.

Incline

Things that gesture toward a corkscrew
include the duck penis, a sine

wave with complex numbers
along the imaginary axis, digital signal

processing for continuous variables like voice
and temperature, scroll

violin pegs and other violence
the natural world is tuned towards, wine

bottle openers, the mortal coil
I shuffle down as this virus winds through me,

fusilli noodles in chicken soup tubs you make
twenty-one trips for until you catch

this from me, a twist
you might have seen

labeled as rotini, but I think I'd know
after eating it on the floor from vertigo, alone

but not alone, Finnish ice breakers
or hand augers from the travel

show we drill through while I soup,
and other mechanical motions

where a gentle slope allows a thread
to run along a matching thread.

Shine

Elephants get drunk from marula
plums that drop and then
rot. Sherry is considered mother's
ruin, made to send empty
barrels to Scotland. Plague doctors
in the Black Death use their beaks
for juniper berries in gin. Deer
are intoxicated by fermented apples.
Like frost, golden resin, dew, I know
what it's like to have fallen,
to spoil on Eden, overnight.

The Pits

Your hands are prunier and bigger than mine
but I can hurt you

anyway isn't that wild my flame-
haired Orpheus will be

gone before the summer
apricots come in so

I guess you'll never try this season's
cake with olive oil

and almond and orange
blossom.

Dramatic Monologue as Clara Rockmore

The dictator is swimming in the peeling orange
and blue under the surface of the skin

of a frozen lake. There's a thickened middle
where it's nighttime

for a follower, tortured in ways
you only read in the history books, or Tolstoy.

By man, quickly and meant
to resemble meat, or by animals,

nibbling slowly. By the light
of a bonfire, and always

left to time and worse,
public exposure. By the last trip-

tych, the gesture repeats. From the depths
towards the light, the dictator is now

and tomorrow, swimming
neck-broken. You wanted to go somewhere

that wasn't there.

Fare

You always have something in store
for me. Bad news.

Leopard pears. Spotty
connections. Your thanksgiving

won't include me. Second year's
less something. Your mother's mastectomy.

Your mother's hip. Your father's spotty
memory. Me, with not enough

produce this year. Stuck in
customs. Your father wants Popeyes

for his heart attack. I produce some
fused Cajun birds. You choose Labor

Day weekend for a cock-up. Bad
pairings. Snow leopards going south

and you. Me
begrudging the Nashville blues.

Dramatic Monologue as Suzanne Ciani

You know when you're going grocery
shopping in the aquatic world and you
have to take your submarine to the
car wash because it's getting dusty.
In the pre-paint world, inside you
there are two water wolves. One a
pastry chef. The other the secretary
of transportation, Bubble Gum Barbie truck
and wig. I could've gone for more depth
sounding, like asunder, pursued
bathymetry to map the seafloor by
dropping the heavy things. Lead, guilt
for setting the fire or having a good time
with taken people. Useless fields to look back on.

Dramatic Monologue as claire rousay

The frequent flying gardener calls it the sexual tension
between wanting to be pollinated and Eden

your next victim. The lanky flowers draw
bees. A medical textbook draws a four-chambered heart

tethered to a dharmachakra mudra. Next
to a Pacman swallowing a Venus

flytrap, which your best friend snaps
the flower buds off of, and calls

the eunuchs of her court, compelling
them to stay. Be forever young.

Morel

Living with you feels like living
in a house-red house, in the Swedish countryside,

with dalmatian mushrooms
and wet orange chanterelles

but there's a penny bun sun
more than three hours a day. Mars' moon

Phobos looks like a mother
of pearl oyster shell.

I don't need a one-armed horse lifter
to tell me why

the monk and the diver
don't make it.

On a List of Games That Buddha Would Not Play, Number 12

Mokkhacika / turning somersaults
men ask who I have / to blow around
here for some good service

men like silver frogs / rotate over axes
for a quick security check / I'm
not a bot. I oversee this dinner as

an abject china doll / men like
axes / splay me / I'm tossed like
greens / frogs (plurality wins / and is

applied equally) / like dressing / on
salad, on display / on my body, the
prone table / the sex addict eats off

on crones' sex and the city. / The recipe
for frog legs begins: snip each apart.
Some people are sex and love

addicts and I might be too, even
though I'm an extra / virgin
olive oil / rawest when it's neon

when I beat off. Shrug off making love
or more money, / and open an account
to take feet pics. / My roommate studies

applied math / on which my ex slaps
the label *selling out* / his father's a hedge
funder. Another outing for a check.

I saw him when he came / and he's
silver / like china left / unfired in the
kiln. / It's dirty work / to make a killing

to clay mask and colloidal silver it up
it'll keep / like 80s housewives love
to say / never I want / and I want

to tell them, eat your princes
for lunch, basted with garlic and
butter. Refrigeration is a damn

new miracle. Now, porcelain's an old
throwdown. So easily impressed
when wet / so easy / to see through

when turned / off I go / drier than the
Gobi Desert / did that just / for you,
everyone / spends for the Sahara. I wish

I were still / unfired, toes limber
enough for five-finger shoes / without
laughing / hard enough / to puke.

Comes up a bit Rorschach / tadpole
like the human / verification. I keep
choosing / the wrong frog.

Dramatic Monologue as Annea Lockwood

Put the tree frogs
inside the drowning piano
and they will play cricket with English

willow mallets and twine balls
around your head. Put a geyser in
the planted piano and it will turn

into a spring peeper's chord data.
Go to sleep inside the piano, and come out
a shining gong. I was about to write

some vertebrates can stop their hearts
beating altogether. Hear
the tines as they rest. Lucky.

Chinese Remainder Theorem

A colloid is a united state
of matter suspended

in another. A hug from a terrycloth mother
preferred over the one wired

with food and drink. I don't think
I want to have the child.

Chemtrails (overblown by now),
milk (fat in liquid, maternal

virus antibodies), Styrofoam nubs
(packing peanuts), slimy mayonnaise

(gross but love), semen.
The difference

between medicine and poison
is dosage. Now a chemist for Dow,

your former aikido teacher
threw you across the room. You can't stop

talking about catching air.
When a pregnant character shows

on TV, you ask if there's anything I need
you to know, and should you set up

a financial plan. Two beautiful islanders
split like pea soup, and online

fans are sad they're not pretending to stay together
for the children. Netflix censors semen,

even when it's indistinguishable from vodka
in a lab cup.

If Neo Has a Belly Button Who's on the Other End of the Umbilical Cord

We take turns / taking pains
on the days we stomach together. / You're in
prime / puking condition

after a bloody-nippled marathon.
Idols are made / in amniotic fluid, clay
and Tough Mudder USA.

If you don't / bug out
when a squirming shrimp
wriggles into the superhero's umbilicus,

you can withstand my public speaking
on why babies are parasites.
Under the covers, I grew up / praying

the late night news wouldn't find me
with their nightly bedbug / eating quota.
You hide from me / your pillbox

of an innie / and I'm already
the depression of a good fender
bender. What a rotten dream / I had

a dreamsicle. With you / I'd like to be
coppertops / or unicorned,
traffic cones on our heads

to spar / in a tunnel. Like a Czech lingerie model,
you want your navel / surgically removed.
Those cylindrical orange ones are

going for 80 to 122 each / once I looked
up the nightmarish price
of a highway barrel. It was going

to be your present. The belly button
gets airbrushed / on
the idol / in post. Real body / horror.

Dramatic Monologue as Maryanne Amacher

It's the spaceship of your parents'
generation—dark glass in the dark

glass that is / the galaxy. Plus
didgeridoo. I want to be heard

like a fragile hyperplane. I'm trying to hand you off
like an earbud / of what it's like being out

here. No multi partners in the higher dimensional
space. You know we were there

in the Middle / East because all the songs
from the millennium / incorporated

the scales. I dabble in the otoacoustic / particularly
the third ear / when it wants to stop

by for a mike / or generate its own
womping reality. There's just a lot going

on / shrinking aches and harbored underwater
eavesdropping / that a glowing brain misses

from earth. Even while on earth.

Capsicum Chinense

Before I get there, you don't stop taking
unnecessary showers

even though they give you ear infections that scar
and you can't afford a doctor right now.

You sent me home with a fist
of a baggie of Scotch bonnets

yellow hot as the sun, as in capsaicin,
as in daisies. I'm allergic to the sticky

sweet pollen. It's meant to be
a beret but I see a cardiac muscle.

The way you wait for the bloodgood maples
of the puzzle when I want a second chance

at childhood, despite your OCD killing you
wordlessly. We don't say we're in it

together, still, you behave more so
than many people I know

who say they love and want each other
and don't want

the yo-yos, or other things that come
with strings. Not to play a tiny violin,

but that condition might be nice
on Valentine's Day. That would be pretty

sick. It's "Paradise (Central
Park)" edition we play, tight, interlocking,

heirloom-quality. All 500 pieces never
repeated. I want us. I want us not

to inherit whatever our parents passed on.
No pressure here. No inflammation.

Dramatic Monologue as Delia Derbyshire

In my best nightmare, I'm not a lizard
brain anymore. It's not an antediluvian flood

while I bob for basement windows.
No scaly Godzilla tracking me through the maze.

The best is when I'm a red-handed
hatchet. I'm not scared of gunmen

or men. It doesn't matter how slowly I walk
or what I wore to the office. I'm smashing

the exit sign. Extinguisher boxes. Breaking
for breaking's sake.

I hesitate to sacrifice Abrahamically and a fellow secret
agent gets it, closes the elevator door

on herself and two children, sending them to the ground
floor where there's a fire I started.

My therapist asks why my expression
is so violent. She asks what happens to the children. I don't know

and I don't care. I don't judge
in the dream. I have goals and I'm checking

boxes. She says I am
the children. I am not. I'm me. She says

I am the other woman,
I am the two children, this is the manifestation

of my psyche. It is all me. I am the burning
building. As in a good program, no one's

coming after me.
I am the end.

ACKNOWLEDGMENTS

Thanks to the editors of the following journals in which some of these poems first appeared: *American Poetry Review, Barrow Street, Bennington Review, Denver Quarterly, Ecotheo, Electric Literature, Gulf Coast, Image, Lana Turner, Maine Review, Mumber Mag, Narrative, New Delta Review, The New Republic, PANK, Poetry, The Poetry Review, Prairie Schooner, Quarterly West, Tagvverk, Tahoma Literary Review, Vassar Review*, and *Yalobusha Review*.

Many thanks to my teachers, my family, and my friends.

PRINCETON SERIES OF CONTEMPORARY POETS

GPSR Authorized Representative: Easy Access System Europe - Mustamäe tee 50, 10621 Tallinn, Estonia, gpsr.requests@easproject.com